Surplus

Spider Silk

Spider

by

AUGUSTA GOLDIN

Thomas Y. Crowell Company

Silk

Illustrated by

JOSEPH LOW

New York

LET'S-READ-AND-FIND-OUT SCIENCE BOOKS

Editors: *DR. ROMA GANS*, Professor Emeritus of Childhood Education, Teachers College, Columbia University

DR. FRANKLYN M. BRANLEY, Chairman of The American Museum—Hayden Planetarium, consultant on science in elementary education

*AVAILABLE IN SPANISH

4   5   6   7   8   9   10

Spider Silk

Spiders are spinners of silk.

During the year the female spider lays a mass of eggs and spins a silk cocoon around them. Baby spiders hatch inside the cocoon.

When they are ready to come out, they tear a hole in
the silk.
They push and shove and try to get away.
They try to get away from each other.
They try to get away from the old cocoon.

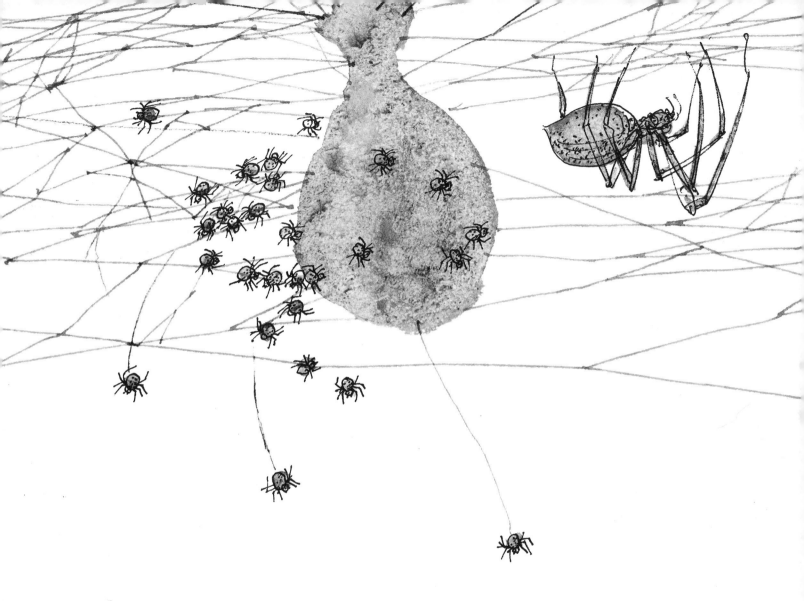

Some of them swing down and away on silk lines.

5

Others wait for the wind to lift
them into the air on silk lines.
When the wind lifts them into
the air, the baby spiders float
like balloons.

Some are tossed over treetops.

Some float over open fields.

Some drift across yards and gardens.

Then they float to the ground.

9

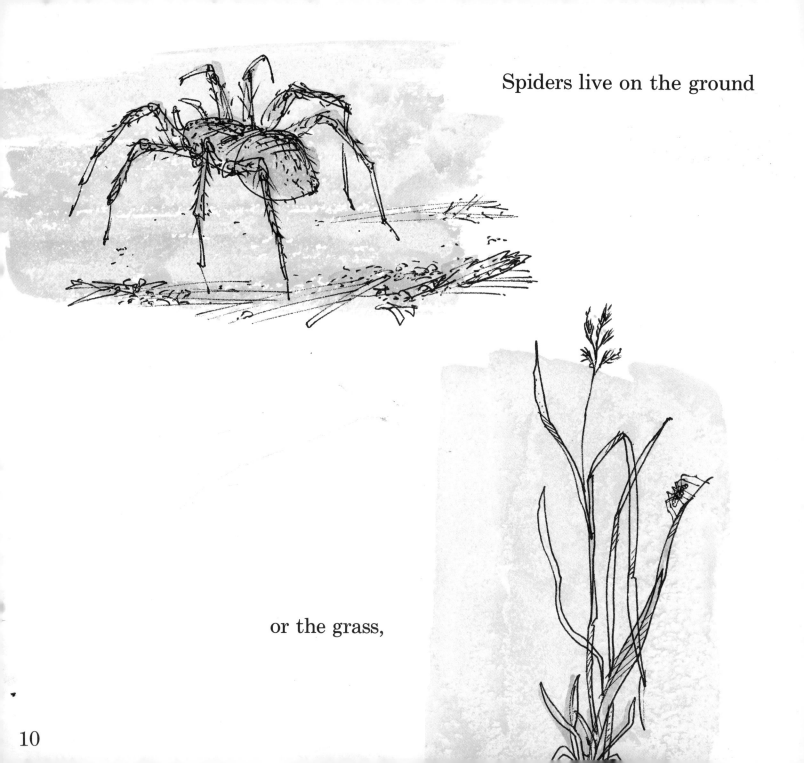

Spiders live on the ground

or the grass,

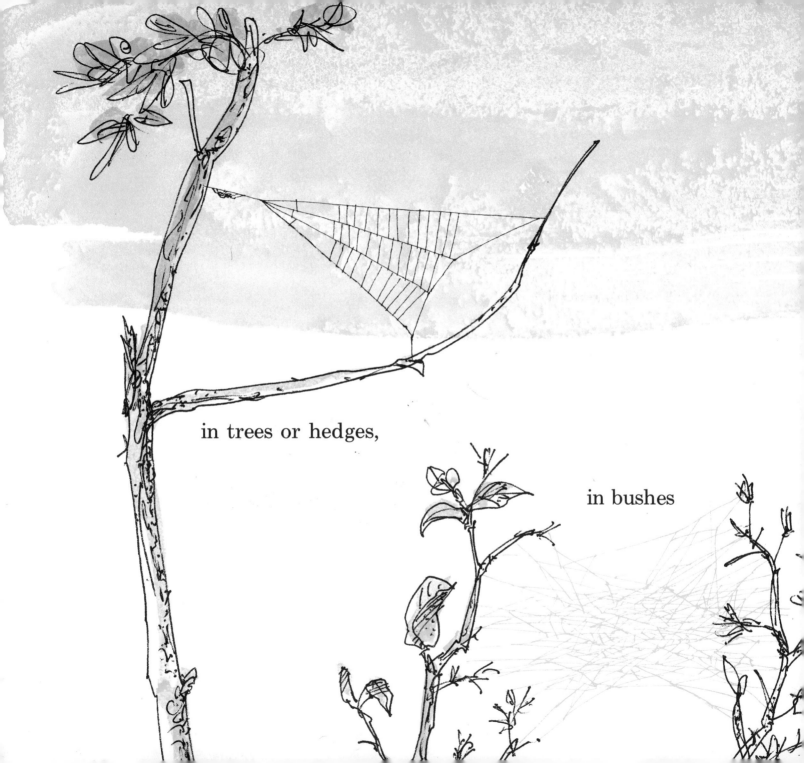

in trees or hedges,

in bushes

or barns

or houses.

Most spiders weave webs wherever they live.
They make their webs of fine silk thread. The webs
   are traps for catching food.

You can find spider webs outdoors and indoors.

Look at windowsills.

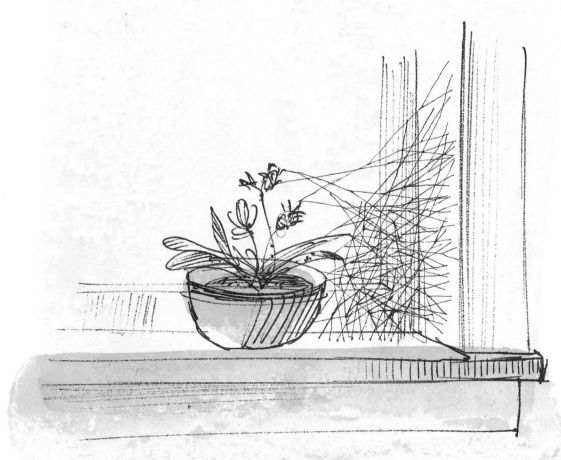

Look in the corners of the cellar or attic.
You may see spider webs.
They are webs made by house spiders.

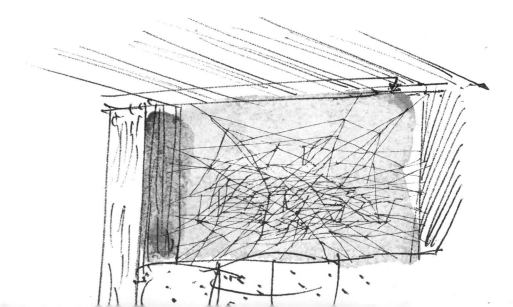

They are blue, like blue smoke.

You can find many kinds of spider webs outdoors.

Some webs are as big as blankets.

Some webs are as little as postage stamps.

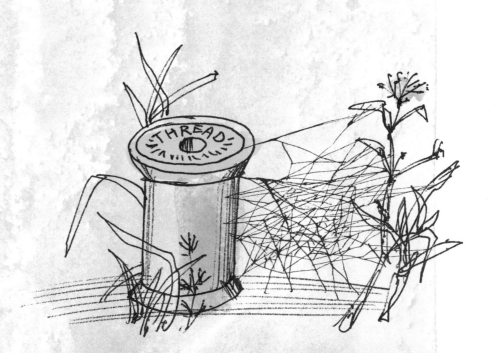

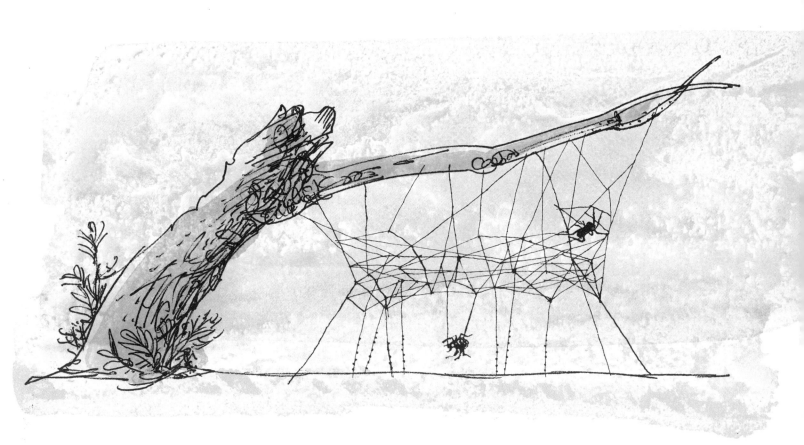

Every single spider web is made of fine silk thread.
Every single web is a trap for flies and mosquitoes,
beetles and bugs—all food for the spider.

Some spiders build webs on the grass.
Look for these webs in the morning when they are
    spangled with dewdrops.
Watch a grass spider build a web.

You will see the spider run this way and that way.
A thread of silk trails out behind the spider.

The silk is hard to see because it is very fine.
If you use a magnifying glass, you can see the silk and
   you can see where the silk comes from. It comes
   from tiny openings at the tip of the spider's body.
Scientists call these openings spinnerets.

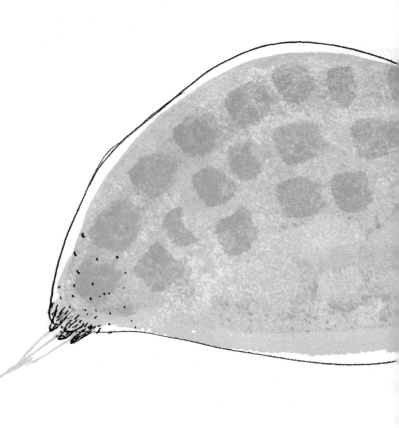

Watch the silk thread come out of the spinnerets.
The thread starts as a fluid inside the spider's body.
The fluid quickly hardens when it hits the air.

Sometimes the spider draws the thread out with its
hind leg.

The grass spider spins this silk thread back and forth
   to build a web on the grass.
Then the spider weaves a silk tube near the web.
The spider hides in the tube and waits for food to be
   caught in the web.

Some spiders build webs on rocks.

A spider building such a web presses its spinnerets to the rock. Then the spider scampers away and the silk line reels out of the spinnerets.

The spider runs back and forth, faster and faster and faster.

The silk threads stick together. They make a little mat.

Soon, flat on the rock, is a sticky, white web.

Ants and beetles will creep into the web. They will be trapped in the sticky silk.

Not all spiders build webs on grass or on rocks.

Hammock spiders build their webs on bushes and hedges.

The webs look like little hammocks swinging from the twigs.

Hammock spiders hang upside down under their webs. They wait for insects to fly into their webs.

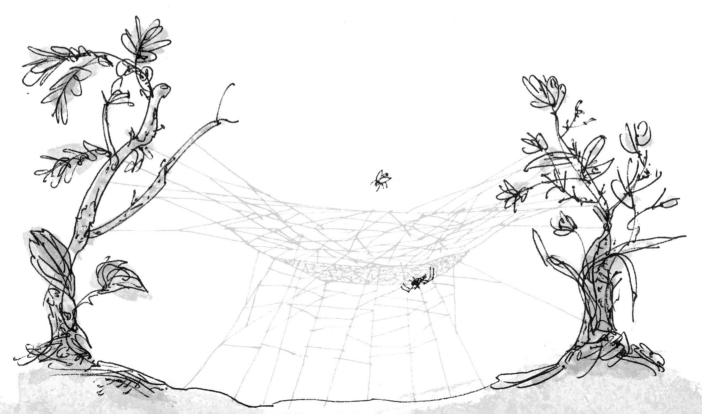

Spider silk looks fine but it is very strong.

It is strong enough to trap a big beetle. It is strong enough to trap a lively grasshopper. Spider silk is strong. It stretches like a rubber band. You can see this for yourself.

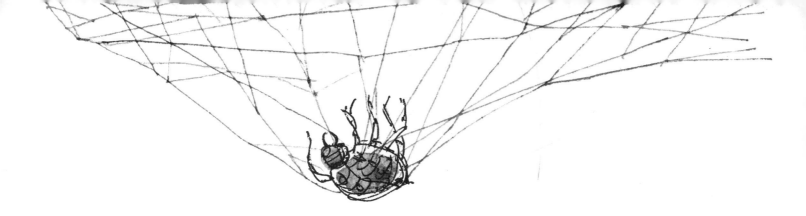

Toss a small beetle into a spider web. The silk threads
   will stretch. The web will sag under the beetle, but
   it will not break.
Toss another beetle into the web.
The web will stretch. It will not break.
If you toss in a large beetle, the web may break.

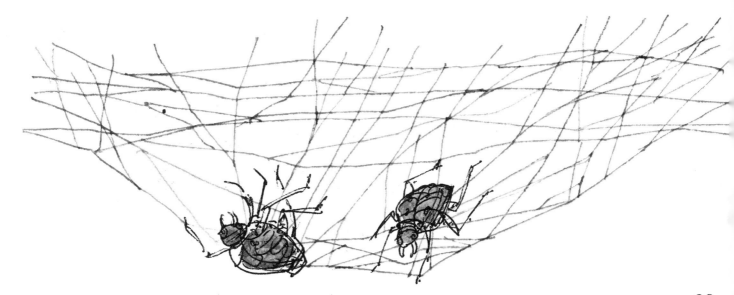

If the web breaks, the spider will mend it carefully by replacing the torn threads. The spider will run back and forth over the torn web. New silk threads will stick to the web. The web will be strong again.

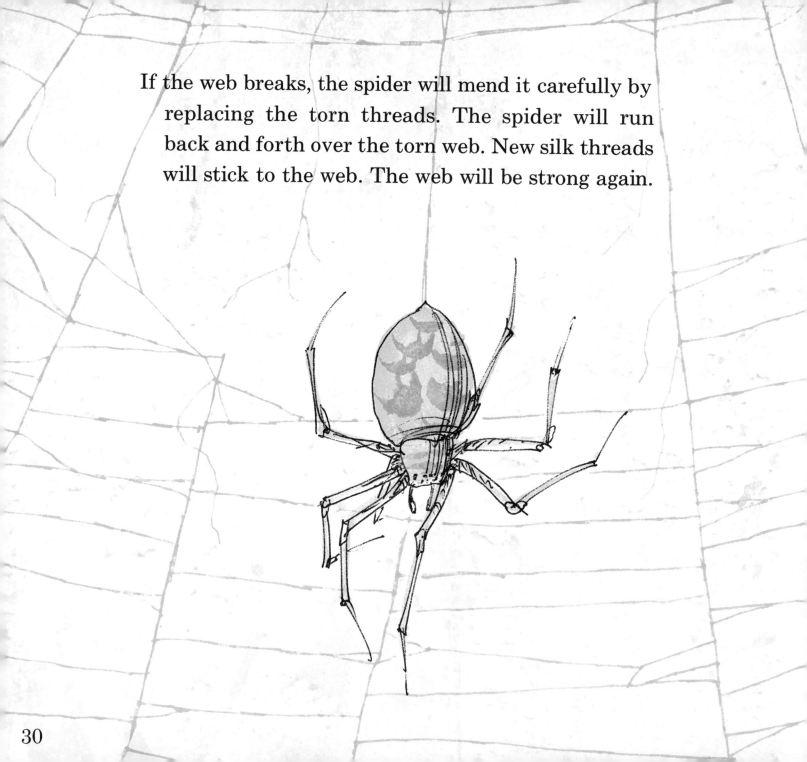

One of the strongest spider webs is an orb web.
It is called an orb web because orb means "circle."
The orb web looks like a wheel made of fine lace.
It begins with a bridge line.
Orb spiders stretch their lacy webs between trees,
between gateposts, and even across running brooks.
The wind may blow leaves and dust and tiny pebbles
into these lacy webs, but they will not break.
An orb can swing in a hurricane and will not break.

Spiders use their silk in many ways.

They use their silk to keep from falling. Gently push
a spider off a twig. The spider will not fall.

It will press its spinnerets to the twig. A strong silk
line will be drawn out of the spinnerets as the
spider swings down.

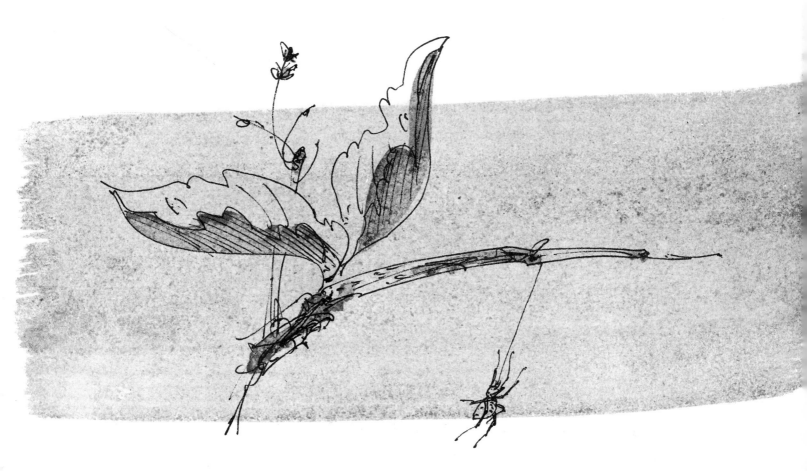

The spider will dangle on the silk line. Then the
spider will climb back up the line to the twig.

A spider uses silk all through life.
It begins life in a silk cocoon.
It weaves silk webs and traps food in them.
A spider swings to safety on a strong silk line.

When it is time for the female spider to lay her eggs
she may lay a hundred tiny eggs. She protects the
mass of eggs with spider silk. She spins a silk cocoon
around them.

Clinging to the remains of her silk web she dies. Her
work in life is done.

About the Author

Augusta Goldin was born in New York City but grew up on a farm in the Catskill Mountains near Ellenville, New York. She was graduated from Hunter College, received a Master of Science degree from the City University of New York, and a doctorate of education from Teachers College, Columbia University.

Mrs. Goldin has worked on the staffs of several education publications and is the principal of a school on Staten Island, New York.

She has traveled around the world and visited Mexico, Canada, and Europe many times. She and her husband live on Staten Island. They have a daughter and a son.

About the Illustrator

Joseph Low was born in Coraopolis, Pennsylvania; attended schools in Oak Park, Illinois; and studied at the University of Illinois. Finding, however, that he could learn more of what he wanted by studying on his own in museums and libraries, he pursued his interest in the graphic arts, teaching himself the skills that he needed and acquiring the necessary tools, type, and a press.

After spending some time at the Arts Students League in New York City, Mr. Low taught graphic arts at Indiana University for three years. He is a printer and publisher, with his own Eden Hill Press, as well as an artist.

His work has been exhibited in museums across the United States, in England, in South America, the Orient, and in Europe. He lives in Connecticut with his wife and two daughters.

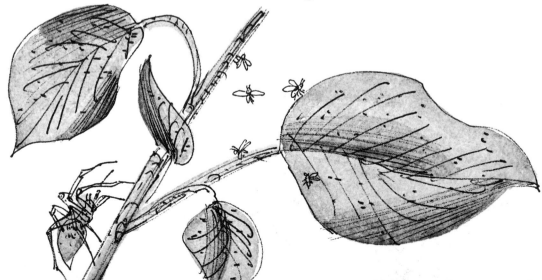